bake me I'm yours...
cupcake

Joan and Graham Belgrove

David and Charles

We would like to dedicate this book to:

Bessie, George, Edna and Frank

A DAVID & CHARLES BOOK
Copyright © David & Charles Limited 2007

David & Charles is an F+W Publications Inc.
company
4700 East Galbraith Road
Cincinnati, OH 45236

First published in the UK in 2007

Text and designs copyright © Joan and
Graham Belgrove 2007
Photography copyright David & Charles 2007

Joan and Graham Belgrove have asserted
their right to be identified as author of this
work in accordance with the Copyright,
Designs and Patents Act, 1988.

The author and publisher have made every
effort to ensure that all the instructions in the
book are accurate and safe, and therefore
cannot accept liability for any resulting injury,
damage or loss to persons or property,
however it may arise.

Names of manufacturers and other products
are provided for the information of readers,
with no intention to infringe copyright or
trademarks.

A catalogue record for this book is available
from the British Library.

ISBN-13: 978-0-7153-2726-5 hardback
ISBN-10: 0-7153-2726-7 hardback

Printed in China by SNP Leefung
for David & Charles
Brunel House   Newton Abbot   Devon

Commissioning Editor Jennifer Fox-Proverbs
Desk Editor Bethany Dymond
Head of Design Prudence Rogers
Art Editor Sarah Underhill
Designer Emma Sandquest
Project Editor Natasha Reed
Production Controller Ros Napper
Photographer Lorna Yabsley

Visit our website at www.davidandcharles.co.uk

David & Charles books are available from all
good bookshops; alternatively you can contact
our Orderline on 0870 9908222 or write to
us at FREEPOST EX2 110, D&C Direct, Newton
Abbot, TQ12 4ZZ (no stamp required UK
only); US customers call 800-289-0963 and
Canadian customers call 800-840-5220.

Contents

cupcake heaven...

Cupcakes are now becoming so popular that they are establishing themselves in many new ways. People are, for instance, sending cupcakes instead of flowers, bringing a box full of cupcakes to a party instead of a bottle, having champagne and cupcake parties, and celebrating all kinds of special occasions, from Baby Showers to Diamond Weddings, with cupcakes. Cupcake tiers are now the new fashion in wedding cakes too.

Cupcakes are without doubt "a cake for all seasons"—universally appreciated by young and old—and so versatile—truly there's a cupcake design for every occasion. You certainly don't need an excuse to indulge in a cupcake, but there are so many occasions at any time of year to celebrate, so why not make the most of them by creating innovative cupcake designs. This book shows you clever ways—some quick, some more detailed—to decorate your cupcakes to turn them into cakes fit for the funkiest teen, poshest wedding, laziest picnic, or any special occasion imaginable.

All you need to know is in here—it is full of ideas which hopefully will inspire you to create your own cupcake designs for whatever the occasion or celebration… and have fun in the process. We hope you will enjoy the pages that follow and more importantly have a go and join in the fun!

bake me...

This section is about mixing and baking the cake batter itself. After all, you have to bake the cakes before you can get on with the fun part of creating designs! Read this part thoroughly and make sure you have all the materials and equipment on hand before you begin.

Basic Equipment...

♡ Food processor, whisk or mixing spoon

♡ Food mixer or hand mixer

♡ Spatula

♡ Measuring spoons

♡ Cooling racks

♡ Cupcake pans

♡ Flour sifter

what you'll need

We'll assume that you have an oven, a refrigerator, a kitchen sink etc—so here are the other basics. Food mixing can be done either by machine or by hand if you don't have an electric mixer.

Cupcake cups and pans

There is a variety of different sizes to choose from, which allows you to try different looks and designs when creating your cupcake masterpieces.

Throughout the book, we use four different sizes of cupcakes:
Very Little—petit four cups
Little—a mini muffin cup size, 1 1/8 in x 1 in

Not So Little—a traditional cupcake cup 1¾ in x 1 1/16 in
Not At All Little—traditional muffin cup

Cupcake pans usually have either 12 or 24 cups. Make sure your paper cups fit snugly into the pan cups.

Fill the paper cups about half full with the cupcake mixture, allowing plenty of room for your cakes to rise to perfection.

You will know when to take your cakes out of the oven, as the center will spring back when touched. Leave the cupcakes to cool in the cupcake pan for five minutes, then transfer to a cooling rack to cool completely—and enjoy!

size matters

Each cake recipe should make one batch of:
48 "Very Little" cupcakes plus a few extra
36 "Little" plus a few extra
24 "Not So Little" plus a few extra, or
12 "Not At All Little" cupcakes plus a few extra.

vanilla cake

1 Preheat the oven to 350°F. Place paper cups in cupcake pans.

2 Put sugar, then flour (sifted), then chopped-up butter and vanilla extract into a food processor. Blitz all together on medium power until well mixed. Alternatively mix it all together with a whisk or spoon.

3 Then add eggs one by one, using a slow pulse setting if using a food processor, until the mix is integrated.

Check out the "flavor me" ideas opposite for delicious alternatives to the basic vanilla cake.

ingredients...

- ♡ 1 cup (8 oz) slightly salted butter
- ♡ 1 cup (8 oz) superfine sugar
- ♡ 4 medium eggs
- ♡ 2 cups (8 oz) self-rising flour
- ♡ 1 tsp natural vanilla extract

The mixture should be a soft dropping consistency when ready to spoon out into baking cups.

4 Spoon the mixture into the cups in the cupcake pan. Place in the center of the oven and bake for:
11–12 minutes ("Very Little")
13–14 minutes ("Little")
15–17 minutes ("Not So Little")
18–20 minutes ("Not At All Little")
Bake for the time mentioned or until the tops of the cakes spring back when lightly touched.

5 Turn out and cool on wire racks.

chocolate cake

1 Preheat the oven to 325°F. Place paper cups in cupcake pans.

2 Put sugar, butter, eggs, and vanilla extract into food processor. Blitz together on full power for a good 2–3 minutes. Remove blade. Alternatively, mix it all together with a whisk or spoon.

3 Sift the flour, baking powder, and cocoa together into a separate bowl and then add to the wet mix gradually, folding in with a spatula.

ingredients...

♡ 3 medium eggs

♡ ¾ cup (6 oz) superfine sugar

♡ 1 cup (4 oz) self-rising flour

♡ 6 tbsp cocoa powder

♡ 1½ tsp baking powder

♡ 1 tsp natural vanilla extract

♡ ¾ cup (6 oz) slightly salted butter

If you are short of time you can buy plain cupcakes from the supermarket or bakery, ready to decorate.

4 Spoon the mixture into the cups.

5 Place in the center of the oven and bake for:
12–13 minutes ("Very Little")
14–15 minutes ("Little")
16–18 minutes ("Not So Little")
20–22 minutes ("Not At All Little")
Bake for the time mentioned or until the tops of the cakes spring back when lightly touched.

6 Turn out and cool on wire racks.

Use the best quality cocoa you can find, ideally Dutch-processed cocoa.

coffee cake
Use the basic vanilla cake recipe but add in 1 tablespoon of strong instant coffee dissolved in 1 tablespoon of milk, and pulse into the mix at the very end.

orange & lemon
Just substitute orange or lemon for vanilla extract in the basic vanilla cake recipe.

lavender
This flavor would work very well for a unique cupcake.

frost me...

The next stage is adding the icing or frosting to your cupcakes. With a little practice, it is easy to achieve a professional-looking iced or frosted finish. None of the projects in this book require any great expertise. If you can roll out pastry and cut out shapes, you will soon do everything else with just a bit of practice.

basic equipment...
- ♡ Smooth nonstick board
- ♡ Rolling pin
- ♡ Flexible plastic spatulas
- ♡ Pastry bags
- ♡ Tips of various shapes
- ♡ Metal spatulas
- ♡ Sieve

flavor me...
Any of the icing and frosting recipes that follow can be easily adapted.

get fruity
Fruity extracts such as lemon and orange add a delicate hint of flavor and are especially perfect for spring and summer creations.

get fresh
Peppermint extract gives a delicious freshness, while rose extract adds a taste of romance.

to get the taste...
Just substitute some of the water (or vanilla extract if buttercream) with the flavoring.

frosting

This is the general term used to describe a smooth, creamy style of icing, achieved by the addition and blending in of butter.

buttercream frosting

1 Beat the butter until soft in a food processor. Alternately use a whisk or spoon.

2 Gradually beat in the confectioners' sugar and water, a little at a time.

3 Continue beating until frosting is light and fluffy.

4 Toward the end, add the vanilla extract.

ingredients...

- ♡ 1 cup (8 oz) unsalted butter
- ♡ 1 tsp natural vanilla extract
- ♡ 4 cups (1 lb) sifted confectioners' sugar
- ♡ 2½ tbsp cold water

chocolate buttercream frosting

1 Sift the cocoa together with the confectioners' sugar.

2 Beat the butter to a cream in a food mixer, or use a whisk or spoon.

3 Alternately add the water and the sugar/cocoa mix, a little at a time, beating together until light and fluffy.

Coffee or chocolate flavoring can also be easily made by dissolving either instant coffee powder or cocoa in hot water and mixing together with the icing.

ingredients...

♡ 1½ cups (6 oz) sifted confectioners' sugar

♡ 4 tbsp cocoa, Dutch-processed if possible

♡ 3 tbsp cold water

♡ ½ cup (4 oz) soft unsalted butter

royal icing

Royal Icing distinguishes itself from other icing by its pure white, smooth finish. This is the best icing to use for piping work on your cakes. Royal icing can be bought from cake-decorating suppliers, but if you want to make your own, here is the recipe.

ingredients...

- ♡ white of 1 medium egg
- ♡ 2 cups (8 oz) sifted confectioners' sugar
- ♡ 2–3 drops of lemon juice

1 Beat egg white until foamy.

2 Gradually beat in confectioners' sugar and lemon juice, and continue beating for five minutes until icing is snowy white.

It is best to use royal icing as soon as it is made because it sets and hardens fairly quickly. If this is not possible, keep the icing covered with a damp cloth until ready for use.

fondant icing

There are two types of fondant icing: pouring and ready-to-roll (see bottom of page). This is the recipe for both.

1 For pouring fondant, you will need a spreading consistency; but the fondant should not be too thin, as it will run too fast to the edges of the cupcake.

For ready-to-roll fondant, make a paste or dough by adding a greater quantity of confectioners' sugar and kneading on a board dusted with confectioners' sugar for 10 minutes.

2 Cover with a clean cloth and leave for half an hour before using.

ingredients...

♡ **2 cups (8 oz) sifted confectioners' sugar (plus extra if making ready-to roll fondant)**

♡ **2–3 tbsp liquid glucose**

♡ **white of 1 medium egg**

For an even finish when applying pouring fondant, smooth out the icing with a flat-bladed knife that has been wetted and excess water shaken off.

pouring fondant

When used as a pouring fondant, this icing gives a better, smoother satin finish to the tops of cupcakes, when compared to, say, glacé icing, which is simply confectioners' sugar mixed with hot water. It is now becoming widely available to buy in ready-to-mix packs, but we have also included the recipe above.

ready-to-roll fondant

This is the same as pouring fondant icing but is made thicker and kneaded into a paste or dough. We, however, have chosen to use ready-made rolled fondant in this book.

petal paste

This, in simple terms, is just like ready-to-roll fondant but hardens quickly and is useful as a modelling paste for making delicate shapes. Petal paste, sometimes referred to as sugar florist paste or modelling paste, can, of course, be made from scratch, but we would recommend the ready-made products for their convenience.

ingredients...

- ♡ **2 cups (8 oz) sifted confectioners' sugar**
- ♡ **2–3 tbsp liquid glucose**
- ♡ **1 tbsp powdered gelatine**
- ♡ **1 tsp glycerine**
- ♡ **1 egg white**
- ♡ **Food coloring as desired**

1 To make, follow the method for royal icing and then knead on a board dusted with cornstarch for 10 minutes. Confectioners' sugar can tend to dry the petal paste out too much if used on the rolling pin and board.

2 Add more confectioners' sugar if necessary to get the consistency of a dough. To get a really smooth, flat, round disk of icing on top of your cupcake, make sure cupcakes are really cooled and, if the cake is rounded on top, shave the center flat with a sharp knife.

Coloring for icing and frosting is available in various forms—e.g. liquid and paste. Use a toothpick to add a little color at a time so you don't overdo it.

adorn me...

Decorating your cakes can be really simple by just adding a variety of different embellishments, as the projects throughout this book show.

decorations and embellishments

Having a large stock of different sprinkles, sparkles, and novelty toppings is the key to cupcake making! Although there is a huge variety in your local supermarket and specialist shops, use the internet for further choice. There's an incredible range to choose from, and you don't have to buy huge quantities to get hold of them.

fake it...

Embellishments don't always have to be edible. Candles, cocktail umbrellas, miniature statues, and other items can be used to turn your cupcake into a work of art. Be careful with nonedible items when serving the cakes; make sure no children can choke on small objects or knock candles over to start a fire.

Some of the techniques in this book call for a bit of patience and precision. But if that's not for you—do your own thing.

Plan ahead in order to coordinate the colors of the icings, frostings, and sprinkles—whether it's a pastel color scheme or a snazzy, glitzy theme.

When adding candy or embellishments to cupcakes, it is best if the icing has set slightly but is still tacky enough to make sure the topping won't fall off.

Sprinkles don't have to be applied individually—just pour a lot of them into a shallow dish and then tip your cupcakes upside-down onto them.

the perfect cup

Cupcake cups, while they might not seem too important, are a big part of your cake design. Just like decorations, the right cup can make or break the look of your cake. There is a huge variety of cups available, from themed seasonal cups to glitzy gold or silver foil cups. So take the time to hunt around for a cup that will suit the theme you are aiming for with the cupcake design.

eat me...

i ♡ valentine

Roses are red, violets are blue, but if cupcakes always do it for you... just enjoy!
These vanilla cupcakes are sweet in more ways than one with delicious
buttercream frosting and delicate heart motifs.

for 36 cakes...

- ♡ 1 batch of Little vanilla cupcakes in red foil cups
- ♡ ½ batch of buttercream frosting
- ♡ ½ batch of royal icing
- ♡ thin tipped pastry bag
- ♡ nonstick baking paper

1 Make the hearts the night before. Keeping the line continuous, pipe out heart shapes onto nonstick baking paper with the royal icing. Leave to set.

2 Carefully peel off in the morning and leave on a flat, clean surface until ready to use.

3 Pipe a generous swirl of buttercream frosting onto the cupcakes and gently push the heart shapes into position.

lovers' tip

If you don't have time to pipe the hearts then just make the hearts out of petal paste and cut out with a heart-shaped cutter (right).

back to basics vanilla cupcakes p8... buttercream frosting p12... royal icing p14...

come in for coffee

All dark and sultry—an irresistible combination of moist, rich chocolate cake with a two-tone coffee and chocolate frosting, topped with a chocolate-coated coffee bean... who needs after-dinner mints when you've got these?

for 36 cakes...

- ♡ 1 batch of Little chocolate cupcakes in black foil cups
- ♡ 1 batch of frosting, divided to make chocolate and coffee flavors
- ♡ large star tipped pastry bag
- ♡ chocolate-coated coffee beans
- ♡ cocoa powder

1 Pipe the chocolate frosting in a large swirl all over the cakes; then apply a smaller swirl of coffee frosting onto the center of each cake, using a similar tip.

2 Gently push a couple of the coated coffee beans into the middle, just enough to secure them.

3 Finish with a light dusting of cocoa powder—just like on a cappuccino.

a dark secret

Put a generous splash of Tia Maria or Kahlua in when you are making the frosting—wicked!

back to basics chocolate cupcakes p9... frosting p13...

love is in the air

Spring, that time of year when one's thoughts turn to... cupcakes, of course! A light, refreshing mix of pastel colors, conjuring up all things fresh and new. The sweet butterflies add a feminine touch to these cakes.

for 24 cakes...

- ♡ 1 batch of Not So Little vanilla cupcakes in pastel pink cups
- ♡ 1 batch of pink fondant icing
- ♡ small quantity of royal icing, colored pink
- ♡ small silver balls for decoration
- ♡ colored petal paste
- ♡ small tipped pastry bag
- ♡ small heart-shaped cutters, in two sizes

1 Carefully cover each cupcake with a cap of pink fondant icing. Take care to get a nice, even and smooth finish.

2 For each butterfly, use petal paste and small heart-shaped cutters in two different sizes to form the wings on each side.

3 Pipe the rest of the butterfly's body with royal icing and finish with small silver balls.

refreshing tip
Develop your springtime theme with other flora and fauna shapes, simply pressed out of colored petal paste.

back to basics vanilla cupcakes p8... fondant icing p15... petal paste p16...

chocolate lover

Anyone with a sweet tooth will have fallen in love with a cake at least once in their lives, and will find themselves head over heels for the rich chocolate sponge and decadent frosting of these tempting cupcakes.

for 24 cakes...

- ♡ 1 batch of Not So Little chocolate cupcakes in red foil cups
- ♡ 1 batch of chocolate frosting
- ♡ large star tipped pastry bag
- ♡ red sugar hearts
- ♡ red sugar sprinkles

1 Pipe the frosting in large swirls onto the cakes; make sure you do this slowly to ensure a generous portion on each.

2 Gently push a sugar heart into the top, just enough to secure it.

3 Add sprinkles around the heart, ensuring that plenty of the luscious chocolate frosting is still visible!

lovely idea
If you make these for a winter wedding, try using gold cups and sprinkles to give the rich chocolate a sumptuous shimmer.

back to basics chocolate cupcakes p9... chocolate frosting p13...

engagement bling

You've got a big event to celebrate, so make an impact with this stunning yet simple design that is sure to be a big hit.

for 36 cakes...

♡ 1 batch of Little vanilla cupcakes in silver foil cups

♡ 1 batch of fondant icing

♡ small quantity of petal paste

♡ small circular cutters

♡ assorted sizes of silver or colored ball decorations

♡ edible silver or gold paint

♡ edible glue

1 Carefully ice the top of each cake with a neat circle of fondant icing and allow to set. Take care not to make the mixture too thin.

2 Make the ring band out of thinly rolled petal paste, using two concentric circular cutters, and then paint with edible silver paint (or gold if you prefer).

3 Apply the ball decorations, securing in place with edible glue, to complete the ring.

engaging thought

This design is very color versatile and can be easily adapted to coordinate with the colors of the real engagement ring!

back to basics vanilla cupcakes p8... fondant icing p15... petal paste p16...

black satin

Who would have thought a cupcake could remind you of sexy lingerie and black satin sheets! These scintillating cupcakes are bound to get you in the right mood to celebrate with that special someone.

for 36 cakes...

♡ 1 batch of Little vanilla cupcakes in red foil cups

♡ black ready-to-roll fondant icing

♡ royal icing

♡ pink coloring

♡ pastry cutter

♡ heart-shaped decorations and small silver balls

♡ small tipped pastry bag

1 First of all roll out the black ready-to-roll fondant icing, cut out the circles with a pastry cutter, and then place on the cupcakes.

2 Mix royal icing with a little pink coloring to achieve a medium pink color and then pipe three long thin lines.

3 Finish the design with alternating red hearts and small silver balls.

wedding bells
Create this design in pretty whites and pinks or blues for a more innocent take on the theme for a bridal shower.

back to basics vanilla cupcakes p8... royal icing p14... ready to roll icing p15...

more cupcakes for...

anniversaries

Celebrate these special wedding anniversaries with mouth-watering cupcakes personalized for the occasion.

first of many

This a paper anniversary, so why not use rice paper to create some heart-shaped decorations, but don't forget to make it 366 if it's a leap year.

sleek silver

Lengths of very thin rolled icing, cut into strips like ribbon pasta and beautifully decorated, can create a stunning effect for this all-important event.

tip to remember

Edible writing pens can sometimes be an easier option than piping. We used them on the "first of many" cupcake (left).

ruby bubbly

The chink of glasses is always a nice way to celebrate. Capture the bubbliness of champagne with this design or choose different shapes of glasses or colors of drinks to match your favorite tipple.

bold gold

This truly memorable occasion is deserving of some pretty memorable cakes. When grouped together like this, metallic balls create real impact.

cocoa loco

A big splash of color swimming in chocolate is the general idea here… chocolate drops, fruit candies, and jelly sweets all work well to make a colorful display.

for 36 cakes...

- ♡ 1 batch of Little chocolate cupcakes in dark brown cups
- ♡ 1 batch of chocolate frosting
- ♡ metal spatula
- ♡ plentiful supply of colorful chocolate or fruit sugar-coated candies

1 Smooth a generous circle of chocolate frosting onto each cupcake and flatten into a very shallow swirl with a metal spatula.

2 Separate out your colored candy decorations beforehand, particularly if you are making a lot of cupcakes, all with the same pattern.

3 Gently position the candies into the arrangement of your choice.

bright idea
Leave the decorations to the last minute as some of them will absorb moisture and may crumble or lose their brightness if left too long before they're eaten.

back to basics chocolate cupcakes p9... chocolate frosting p13...

1st birthday

A great way to mark your little one's landmark occasion… just say it with cupcakes.

for 36 cakes...

- ♡ 1 batch of Little vanilla cupcakes in red foil cups
- ♡ ½ batch of fondant icing
- ♡ ½ batch of royal icing
- ♡ food coloring
- ♡ thin tipped pastry bag

1 Carefully ice the top of several cupcakes with a neat circle of brightly colored fondant icing and allow to harden off for at least an hour.

2 Make the royal icing to the right consistency for piping letters and numbers. Pipe one per cupcake, and arrange on platters or tiers.

no.1 tip
If you have a mixed group of adults and children coming to the celebration, make up some larger cupcakes as well to match the designs of the smaller versions.

back to basics vanilla cupcakes p8... royal icing p14... fondant icing p15...

candy store

These irrestistible treats conjure up wonderful images of candy shops… for you and the kids! This is one design you don't need to spend time carefully arranging.

for 36 cakes…

♡ 1 batch of Little vanilla cupcakes in brightly colored cups

♡ 1 batch of buttercream frosting

♡ large star tipped pastry bag

♡ small fork

♡ buckets of your child's favorite mini candies

♡ food coloring

1 Divide your frosting batch into smaller batches so you can make up several different colors.

2 Place a generous swirl of frosting on the cupcake and then scatter on the candy topping.

3 Use a small fork to work in some of the candies and then scatter on a few more.

quick dip

Just tip their favorite miniature candies into bowls, turn your ready-frosted cupcake upside-down and dip!

back to basics vanilla cupcakes p8… buttercream frosting p12…

make a face

Kids can join in or take the lead here... just set them up with lots of edible bits and pieces and some plain fondant iced cakes, they won't need much teaching to create scrumptious-looking smiley faces!

for 24 cakes...

♡ 2 batches of Not At All Little cupcakes in plain or pastel cups

♡ 2 batches of fondant icing

♡ icing color

♡ quantities of candies the kids can use to make eyes, noses, mouths, hair, and so on

1 Prepare the face decorations. Be careful to avoid using anything children might possibly choke on.

2 Using the larger cupcakes allows children the most room to be creative. Spread a disk of fondant icing onto each cupcake, colored enough to represent skin color, and set aside.

3 Round up the kids and, after giving them a short demonstration, retire to a safe place...

let's face it

It's probably a good idea to give each child their own little stock of items for face decorations.

back to basics vanilla cupcakes p8... fondant icing p15...

rocky mountain

Ideal for kids' bonfire nights and halloween parties, these look absolutely sumptuous and are bound to leave them all speechless... for a nice change!

for 24 cakes...

- ♡ 1 batch of Not So Little chocolate cupcakes in plain dark brown or brightly coloured cups
- ♡ 1 batch of chocolate frosting
- ♡ metal spatula
- ♡ melted chocolate (dark or milk to your taste)
- ♡ mini marshmallows and popcorn

1 Apply a generous swirl of chocolate frosting to each cupcake and spread around with a metal spatula.

2 Start building up your 'mountain of rocks' with an assortment of popcorn and marshmallows, securing them in the frosting as you go.

3 Finish with a generous drizzle of chocolate, and serve immediately.

rock solid tip
Although you can, of course, melt chocolate over the top of these, it's just as effective and much less bother to use the squeezy chocolate sauce, but watch out for messy fingers!

back to basics chocolate cupcakes p9... chocolate frosting p13...

sugar and spice

These multicolored sweets are so versatile and can be sliced or broken into all kinds of shapes. Add a dusting of sugar to make the cupcakes shimmer and sparkle—these pretty creations are definitely what little girls are made of!

for 36 cakes...

- ♡ 1 batch of Little cupcakes in brightly colored cups
- ♡ 1 batch of buttercream frosting
- ♡ knife
- ♡ an assortment of multicolored candies, ready sliced or broken into different shapes
- ♡ colored sugar sprinkles
- ♡ food coloring

1 Cover each cupcake generously with tinted buttercream frosting and draw up into small peaks with a knife.

2 Press in and arrange sweets to make an attractive display of color.

3 Finish off with a scattering of colored sugar sprinkles.

oh so pretty

We've used pink and yellow colored cups in the picture. Try a selection of the many pastel-colored cups now available for that extra touch of sweetness.

back to basics vanilla cupcakes p8... buttercream frosting p12...

more cupcakes for...

new arrivals

A new addition to the family is a real cause for a celebration! These unique cupcakes will be the talk of the party and will go perfectly with some bubbly to christen the newborn.

new baby

A fitting way to celebrate such a wonderful event. These elegant little jewels in their individual gift boxes are a perfect choice gift for guests at christenings.

gift wrapped

Why not send your guests home with a cupcake favor bon bon? Wrap in circles of clear cellophane and tie off the top with ribbon.

celebrate the date

Look what the stork has brought! These delicate cupcakes mark that special occasion so beautifully and are a simple yet so pretty way to celebrate your child's christening party. These look superb arranged on pastel china platters or tiers.

mother's day flowers

Moms around the world will really love these pretty cupcakes, and they are bound to appreciate how much effort you have gone to for their special day.

for 24 cakes...

- ♡ 1 batch of Not So Little vanilla cupcakes in pretty colored cups
- ♡ ½ batch of rose-colored royal icing
- ♡ small quantity of petal paste
- ♡ 1 batch of buttercream frosting
- ♡ rose stencil
- ♡ metal spatula
- ♡ round cutter
- ♡ rose-colored sprinkles
- ♡ star tipped pastry bag

1 Pipe a generous swirl of buttercream frosting over each cupcake. Roll out a thin plaque of petal paste, large enough to make several roses at once, and allow to harden off.

2 Make a stiff paste of rose-colored royal icing and, using a metal spatula, spread into stencil while it is placed on the surface of the plaque. Lift off the stencil carefully.

3 Cut out roses with a round cutter and place two on the frosting. Finish with sugar or sprinkles.

mom's the word

For that extra bit of indulgence, try flavoring the frosting with a few drops of rose water after whisking.

back to basics vanilla cupcakes p8... royal icing p14... petal paste p16...

hats off to uncle sam

The 4th of July is a day for family fun. Whether celebrating indoors or outdoors with fireworks and BBQ, these patriotic little cupcakes are sure to please.

for 36 cakes...

- ♡ 1 batch of Little vanilla cupcakes in red foil cups
- ♡ 1 batch of buttercream frosting
- ♡ icing tools or a sharp paring knife
- ♡ petal paste
- ♡ yellow sparkles
- ♡ colored sugar strands
- ♡ edible glitter

1 Using a metal spatula, spread a spoonful of yellow buttercream frosting right to the edges of each cupcake.

2 To make the hat, start with the shape in white and then build the colors on top—first the red stripes and then the blue band and the white star.

3 Finally add glitter to the hat and colored sugar strands and sparkles to the frosting.

independent thought

Stick a miniature indoor sparkler in some of the cupcakes and turn off the lights (don't leave unattended).

back to basics vanilla cupcakes p8... buttercream icing p12...

the graduate

It's an important time in any young person's life—wherever they are graduating from, it's your chance to show them how proud you are of their achievements.

for 24 cakes...

- ♡ 1 batch of Not So Little vanilla cupcakes in plain or foil cups
- ♡ ½ batch of roll icing
- ♡ ½ batch of colored ready-to-roll fondant
- ♡ white petal paste
- ♡ edible ink pen
- ♡ star sprinkles

1 Spread a smooth, neat disk of colored fondant to the edges of the cake.

2 Roll out a thin ribbon of red fondant and place on the cake to look like untied ribbon.

3 Make a diploma scroll from very thinly rolled petal paste, and use an edible ink pen to write the name. Write the words on the scroll before you roll it up and place it on the cake—it's a lot easier. Place on the fondant and finish with a few star sprinkles.

first class
Practice writing with the ink pen before trying it on the scroll, as it can be tricky.

back to basics vanilla cupcakes p8... ready to roll fondant icing p15...

thanksgiving treats

Make sure you have all got room after the turkey for these fruity treats. Give thanks for the harvest by creating these sweet little cakes for the whole family.

for 12 cakes...

- ♡ 1 batch of 12 Not At All Little vanilla cupcakes
- ♡ 14 oz of either canned black cherries (drained) or fresh cherries (stoned)
- ♡ cherry glaze
- ♡ confectioners' sugar for dusting
- ♡ heavy cream, whipped
- ♡ pastry bag and tip

1 Remove the tops of the cakes, taking out a deep circular groove of cake and set aside.

2 Place a few cherries in a little pile in the center of each cupcake and then spoon over the cherry glaze while it is not quite set.

3 Replace the cake tops, shaving off some of the cake underneath so they sit nicely on top. Dust the cupcakes with confectioners' sugar, then finish with a swirl of whipped cream.

harvest display
Try other ideas, such as apple pie filling or any seasonal berries in jam.

back to basics vanilla cupcakes p8...

halloween headline

Never mind the usual ghosts and pumpkins, they will take their hats off to you over these! There is very simple modeling involved in these spooky specimens so you can be as creative as you like.

for 24 cakes...

♡ 1 batch of Not So Little vanilla cupcakes in orange or halloween cupcake cups

♡ ½ batch of fondant icing

♡ black and red rolled fondant icing

♡ bright yellow star sprinkles

♡ pastry tip

♡ edible glitter

1 Spread a plain white fondant icing disk over each cupcake, close to the edges. Using a suitable size pastry tip and the black rolled fondant, fashion the cone of the witch's hat around the tip, allowing enough excess to make the floppy brim.

2 Put a thin red band of rolled fondant icing around the base of the hat.

3 Decorate the hat with several stars, and finish with a scattering of edible glitter.

spooky thought
Try your newfound modeling skills with other shapes... black cats, broomsticks and cauldrons.

back to basics vanilla cupcakes p8... fondant icing p15...

new year, new cupcake

When the clock strikes 12, make sure you have a glass of champagne to hand, as well as one of these delightful celebratory cupcakes.

for 24 cakes...

- ♡ 1 batch of 24 Not So Little vanilla cupcakes in silver-colored cups
- ♡ 1 batch of rolled fondant, colored blue
- ♡ small amount of petal paste
- ♡ edible silver paint
- ♡ edible glitter

1 Apply a smooth disk of blue rolled fondant to each cake to make the face of the clock.

2 Cut small strips of thin petal paste and coat with edible silver paint to make the dial of the clock and the hands pointing to midnight.

3 Finish with multicolored edible glitter.

ring the changes

They don't have to be all the same — use different-colored fondant, chocolate or coffee cake, and bright cups so everyone can choose a different one.

back to basics vanilla cupcakes p8... petal paste p16...

60   a year in cupcakes

more cupcakes for...

springtime

Easter is the perfect occasion to create some scrumptious treats that are tasty and look gorgeous too!

easter bunny

A cute cupcake with little bunnies peeking out will go down well with guests.

in bloom

A lovely way to enhance that springtime feeling when Easter arrives! Try different color combos too.

cheep trick

If you are really short of time, there are some great Easter sprinkles now available, like little chicks and Easter bunnies, all in pastel colours.

in the nest

A traditional favorite—but make sure you make enough because everyone will want at least one!

duck pond

Kids will love these 3-D cupcakes with a cute little trail of ducklings following behind.

tea for two

A traditional design for a very traditional occasion, but these cakes have extra indulgence of icing on the cake as well as cream and fruit below—pure heaven!

for 24 cakes...

- ♡ 1 batch of Not So Little vanilla cupcakes in plain or silver foil cups
- ♡ ½ batch of fondant icing
- ♡ heavy cream, whipped
- ♡ fresh summer berries
- ♡ sprinkles to coordinate with the fruit

1 Spread a neat circle of fondant close to the edge of each cupcake, leaving a border. Allow to harden, covering with sprinkles when almost dry.

2 Cut a complete circle of cake and fondant out of the top of the cake, creating a hollow. Cut the removed cake in two and set aside.

3 Place a generous dollop of whipped cream in each crater and embed a few berries in the cream. Replace the two halves to make butterfly wings and finish with more sprinkles.

dainty idea
Make up a medley of different berries to put on each cupcake.

back to basics vanilla cupcakes p8... fondant icing p15...

hot stuff

Looking just like miniature BBQs themselves, these hot little numbers will go as quickly as hot potatoes... so make sure you make plenty of them! Fiery orange sweets and dark chocolate cookies work best.

for **24 cakes...**

- ♡ 1 batch of Not So Little chocolate cupcakes in dark brown cups
- ♡ 1 batch of chocolate frosting
- ♡ honeycomb and cookies, broken into chunky pieces
- ♡ sharp knife
- ♡ jelly beans or candy corn

1 Spread a base of chocolate frosting onto each cupcake, sufficient to provide a bed for the topping.

2 Arrange broken pieces of honeycomb and cookies to create a "hot coals" effect. For breaking the cookies neatly, use a sharp knife. Despite the use of a knife you don't get clean edges (which you don't want anyway) but you do get pieces of the right size rather than a load of crumbs.

3 Finish with a few jelly beans (the most orangey ones in the bag) or candy corn among them to look like flames.

hot tip
Add fruit on toothpicks to look like fruit kebabs on the BBQ.

back to basics chocolate cupcakes p9... chocolate frosting p13...

dressed for dinner

Your guests will be shaken, if not stirred, by these magnificent after-dinner treats. Suitable for both Bonds and Miss Moneypennys.

for 24 cakes...

♡ 1 batch of **Not So Little** vanilla cupcakes in plain or foil cups

♡ 1 batch of **white rolled fondant icing**

♡ **black petal paste**

♡ **small pearl and silver balls**

♡ **brush**

1 Spread neat circles of white fondant icing—alternatively, choose whatever color suits your color theme—and allow to dry.

2 Make the bow ties and handbags by cutting out of thinly rolled and precolored rolled fondant.

3 Apply to the fondant disc on top of each cake with a damp brush. Finish by adding three pearl balls for the men's bow ties, and silver and a white ball for the ladies' handbags.

perfect host
Place the cupcakes in individual boxes as place settings too.

back to basics vanilla cupcakes p8... rolled fondant icing p15...

double trouble

Everyone will get a big surprise when they bite into these and see the two colors of the cake inside. Try all sorts of color combinations for creative results. Finish with coordinating colored jelly beans for a young-at-heart look.

for 24 cakes...

- ♡ 1 batch of Not So Little vanilla cake mix divided into two
- ♡ food coloring
- ♡ 1 batch of buttercream frosting
- ♡ multicolored jelly beans

1 Divide cake mix in two and color both halves with contrasting food coloring. You will have to use a lot to ensure the colors stand out.

2 Spoon in the cake mix into baking cups, but in two halves, side by side.

3 When baked and cooled, decorate in swirls or peaks with buttercream frosting. Finish with a generous covering of multicolored jelly beans.

that's magic
Always use natural food coloring as you will need to use a lot for bright colors.

back to basics cupcakes p8... buttercream frosting p12...

coffee morning treat

Worth breaking the diet for, these indulgent delights are topped with meringue and sprinkled liberally with two-tone chocolate flakes... delicious!

for 24 cakes...

- ♡ 1 batch of Not So Little coffee cupcakes in patterned cups
- ♡ 1 batch of meringue
- ♡ cappuccino chocolate for grating
- ♡ café curls
- ♡ cocoa powder

1 Smooth a generous layer of whipped meringue over the top of each cupcake and place under the broiler for a few seconds until the meringue has browned on the surface.

2 Allow to cool; then sprinkle shavings of cappuccino chocolate on top and dust with cocoa powder. Finish with half a café curl and serve immediately with your favorite cup of coffee.

meringue mix

To make enough meringue to cover these cupcakes, you will need 3 egg whites, ¾ cup (6 oz) superfine sugar, 1 tsp cornstarch, ½ tsp vinegar, and ½ tsp vanilla extract. Beat the egg whites until very stiff. Then gradually beat in the sugar, cornstarch, vinegar, and vanilla extract. Then spread the meringue in peaks over the cupcakes and place under the broiler long enough to turn the surface peaks golden brown.

back to basics coffee cupcakes p9...

ice cream picnic

When is an ice cream not an ice cream? When it's one of these sugar-plum delights! You'll have great fun making these two-tone toppings, and all the family will be so impressed.

for 24 cakes...

- ♡ 1 batch of Not So Little vanilla cupcakes in pretty patterned cups
- ♡ 1 batch of buttercream frosting, split into two for coloring pink and green
- ♡ large star tipped pastry bag
- ♡ colorful sprinkles
- ♡ ice cream wafers

1 The two-tone effect is achieved by filling the pastry bag with two different colors of frosting. It's a bit tricky to get the two colors side by side in the pastry bag and may take a bit of practice. You must also use quite a big bag and tip.

2 Fill one side of your pastry bag with one of the colors of frosting. Turn the bag around and carefully fill the other half of the bag with the second color. Make a generous two-tone swirl on each cupcake, as you would make a normal swirl. Finish with multicolored sugar or chocolate sprinkles and wafers.

ice idea
Try flavoring the frostings, e.g. with strawberry and mint, for that extra-special treat.

back to basics vanilla cupcakes p8... buttercream frosting p12...

more cupcakes for...

special birthdays

You only have the "big" birthdays once so make sure they go with a bang with fabulous cupcakes.

sweet sixteen

These sweets, cut thinly in cross section, make a lovely colorful display for the youngsters.

eighteen today

This is a very versatile idea—you can use little or even "petit four" size cupcakes to create any word or number, or theme the colors all gold or silver, for example.

timeless tip
Whatever age you are catering for, and whatever design you choose, base it on their favorite type of cupcake or flavor.

twenty-one

Very minimalist but incredibly striking when all grouped together. Make sure you have enough cakes though! Repeat patterns regularly to create a designer effect.

love—forty

Candles on picks look great—forty should be fun after all! Cut the numbers out of petal paste, and for the best effect match the color to the color of your cupcake case.

oriental charm

"3-in-1" pagoda cupcakes are a lot of fun, easy to make, and especially appealing to those members of the family with a hearty appetite!

for 24 pagoda cakes...

- ♡ 1 batch of Not So Little vanilla cupcakes in gold foil cups
- ♡ 1 further batch of vanilla cupcake mix to split between Little and Very Little
- ♡ gold foil cups
- ♡ 1 batch of fondant icing, colored red
- ♡ edible gold glitter
- ♡ angelica

1 Spread a neat circle of colored fondant icing onto the top of each size of cupcake.

2 Before the icing hardens off too much, carefully stack the cakes on top of each other to create your pagoda.

3 Finish by making a roof effect with strips of angelica.

4 Finally, scatter a little edible gold glitter on the exposed icing.

pile up

Try different-colored foil cups—red, silver, and green are readily available—to make a multicolored display.

back to basics vanilla cupcakes p8... fondant icing p15...

island paradise

You can just imagine yourself stretched out on this idyllic little scene, lying under a parasol with your flip-flops kicked off…

for 24 cakes...

- 1 batch of Not So Little vanilla cupcakes in plain cups
- 1 batch of buttercream frosting, colored golden yellow
- small amount of petal paste
- blue and green coloring
- orange sugar
- cocktail umbrellas
- shiny cake-decorating dragées/balls

1 Start your beach scene by covering each cupcake with yellow buttercream frosting.

2 Sprinkle lightly with orange sugar to complete the sunny effect.

3 Cut out sandals from colored rolled petal paste, and then make very thin strips for the thongs.

4 Finally complete the toe decoration with a single same-color shiny dragée and finish with a cocktail umbrella.

sandy tip
Make some variations to this e.g. comb the frosting or make little hills in it to look like sand dunes.

back to basics vanilla cupcakes p8... buttercream frosting p12... petal paste p16...

singing star

Go on, show off your talents with these star-quality designs. These cute cakes are sure to hit the right note.

for 24 cakes...

- ♡ 1 batch of Not So Little vanilla cupcakes in plain cups
- ♡ 1 batch of white fondant icing
- ♡ 1 batch of royal icing, colored black
- ♡ thin tipped pastry bag
- ♡ yellow stars

1 Spread a neat disk of white fondant icing onto each cupcake.

2 When the icing has set a little, pipe the musical staves, notes and treble clef onto the cupcakes.

3 Finish with yellow stars on and around the musical staves.

star turn
Instead of piping, cut out musical shapes and stars from rolled petal paste. You could even make a more 3-D effect by placing them upright in frosting rather than icing.

back to basics vanilla cupcakes p8... royal icing p14... fondant icing p15...

bollywood beauty

Bring a touch of Eastern magic to your cake decorating with this eye-catching paisley design made up of lots of nonpareils and dragées.

for 24 cakes...

- ♡ 1 batch of Not So Little vanilla cupcakes in gold foil cups
- ♡ 1 batch of fondant icing colored pastel pink
- ♡ gold dragées/balls
- ♡ orange and pink nonpareils
- ♡ pastry tip
- ♡ small quantity of royal icing with pink coloring
- ♡ toothpicks
- ♡ paper

1 Make your paisley shape in paper first, to fit the size of the cupcake top and place on the surface. Trace the outline with a toothpick, remove the paper, and then pipe a very thin line of pink royal icing along the outline.

2 Before the piping sets, fix the small gold dragées along the piping line. Repeat the above with the inside paisley pattern shape.

3 Fill in the area inside the gold balls with pink nonpareils. Lightly dampen the icing first with a brush so they will stay in place. Fill the middle with orange nonpareils and add a large gold ball in the center.

spice it up...
Try adding spice into the cake mix—allspice, for example, just ½ tsp per batch.

back to basics vanilla cupcakes p8... royal icing p14... fondant icing p15...

pop your cork

These have a real celebratory feel to them and should definitely be served with champagne, too!

for 24 cakes...

- ♡ 1 batch of Not So Little vanilla cupcakes in gold foil cups
- ♡ 1 batch of buttercream frosting
- ♡ small gold balls/dragées
- ♡ edible gold leaf
- ♡ edible gold paint
- ♡ edible glue
- ♡ petal paste
- ♡ green coloring
- ♡ toothpicks

1 Cover cakes in a thick layer of frosting and finish in small peaks. Color petal paste to the color of a champagne bottle and fashion the top of the bottle.

2 Hollow out the neck with a toothpick, paint with edible gold paint and finish with edible gold leaf. Press into the center of the frosting at an angle.

3 Using edible glue, place some gold balls or dragées down the neck of the bottle. Finish by scattering little gold balls or dragées over the buttercream.

bright ideas...
Different colors can be used to good effect here—pink cases and frosting for pink champagne or gold for Mimosas.

back to basics vanilla cupcakes p8... buttercream frosting p12...

retro look

Even your cupcakes have to keep up with the latest fashion trends… and this dates back to 1960s monochrome looks. Fortunately, minimalist designs are "in" right now so they're not too difficult to reproduce!

for 24 cakes...

- ♡ 1 batch of Not So Little vanilla cupcakes in silver foil cups
- ♡ 1 batch of white rolling fondant icing
- ♡ 1 batch of black rolling fondant icing
- ♡ fondant rolling pin
- ♡ board
- ♡ set each of pastry and small circular icing cutters
- ♡ sharp knife
- ♡ apricot glaze

1 First create a smooth, flat surface to your cupcakes by shaving or slicing off any lumps or bumps with a sharp knife.

2 Apply a light apricot glaze to the surface of the cupcakes so the fondant top you make will stick to it. Make the pattern to your own style, by rolling out the fondant and cutting out different circles and circle rings, interchanging them and pressing in lightly.

3 When your pattern is finished, use a circular cake cutter of the right diameter to cut out a finished top for your cupake.

retro style
For a funky pattern, alternate black and white stripes.

back to basics vanilla cupcakes p8… fondant icing p15…

more cupcakes for...

show-stopping outfits

The most important part of getting ready for a party is your outfit. Accessorize with these sweet treats.

awesome accessory

Use a piece of red rolling fondant just like modelling clay to make your handbag design and bling it up with shiny decorative balls.

dancing shoes

Trace and cut your shoe shapes out of rolled colored fondant or, if you can, make them more 3-D to match the handbag. Use plenty of sugar sprinkles to make them really stunning.

gem of an idea

There are lots of websites now for direct supplies of many different decorations you'll need to create some real razzamatazz for your cupcakes.

bling bling

Paint your decorations with edible glue and glitter to make a large variety of sparkling and colorful baubles for a cake with pizazz.

edible undies

Once you have your basic pants and bustier shapes cut out of fondant, use edible pens and glitter and your imagination to create some lovely patterns and designs. The button on this one has been made by dipping a pearl ball in edible glue and then rolling it in glitter!

shabby chic

Whoever said romance was dead? These sweet little pink hearts are actually really easy and create a vintage romantic setting for the day.

for 24 cakes...

♡ 1 batch of Not So Little vanilla cupcakes in silver foil cups

♡ 1 batch of buttercream frosting

♡ petal paste

♡ food coloring

♡ pink sanding sugar

♡ heart-shaped cutters

1 Roll out a piece of colored petal paste, large enough to make quite a few hearts from the one piece. Using a cutter, make the hearts well in advance and allow to harden.

2 Make the frosting and pipe a generous swirl over each cupcake.

3 Place two hearts at different angles into the frosting swirl and finish with a sprinkle of pink sanding sugar.

chic to chic

You could always pipe your bride and groom initials on each heart to add that final romantic touch.

back to basics vanilla cupcakes p8... buttercream frosting p12... petal paste p16...

spring fresh

These cute butterfly designs will give your wedding day that fresh springtime feel and will complement the sunny weather you have specially ordered for the day.

for 36 cakes...

- ♡ 1 batch of Little vanilla cupcakes in coloured cups
- ♡ 1 batch of fondant icing
- ♡ pastel green and pink coloring
- ♡ petal paste
- ♡ small silver balls
- ♡ small amount of royal icing and coloring
- ♡ thin pastry tip
- ♡ heart-shaped cutters, two different sizes

1 Spread a smooth neat disk of pastel-colored fondant icing to the edges of the cakes and allow to set.

2 Roll out a piece of pale pink petal paste thinly and use two different sizes of heart-shaped cutters to make the wings.

3 Place wings on each cake and, using a thin tip, pipe the body and antennae with royal icing.

4 Finish the tips of the antennae with silver balls.

flutter by
Use flower cutters for a country garden theme.

daisy chain

These cute cupcakes look so indulgent, but they are really simple to make and your guests will absolutely love them.

for 24 cakes...

- ♡ 1 batch of Not So Little vanilla cupcakes in gold foil cups
- ♡ 1 batch of butter frosting
- ♡ small amount of white petal paste
- ♡ daisy cutter
- ♡ coral nonpareils
- ♡ edible gold paint
- ♡ coral decorative sugar
- ♡ star tipped pastry bag
- ♡ fondant rolling pin
- ♡ edible glitter

1 Make butter frosting and, using a star tip and pastry bag, pipe a generous crisscross swirl (like a braid) on each cupcake. Roll out a thin piece of white petal paste, press out daisies with a cutter, and allow to harden.

2 Brush the center of the daisy with edible glue and place five or six of the coral nonpareils in the middle of each daisy. Brush the petals with edible gold paint and sprinkle edible glitter on them while still damp.

3 Place the daisies on the cupcakes. Finish off by sprinkling with coral decorative sugar.

color swatch
These gorgeous cakes also look fab when contrasted with silver daisies.

back to basics vanilla cupcakes p8... buttercream frosting p12... petal paste p16...

chocolate radiance

So informal, yet so temptingly delicious! These fab cakes will look absolutely gorgeous on the day. You'll have to be quick to make sure you get one before they all disappear!

for 24 cakes...

- ♡ 1 batch of Not So Little chocolate cupcakes in dark brown cups or dark patterned cups
- ♡ 1 batch of chocolate frosting
- ♡ selection of chocolate cigarillos
- ♡ white chocolate curls
- ♡ star tipped pastry bag

1 Make chocolate frosting and pipe a generous swirl on each cupcake. Make sure there is enough so that the cupcake looks really luscious.

2 Next, arrange a selection of varied chocolate cigarillos, like crisscrossed logs, on top of the cupcake.

3 Add a light sprinkle of gold glitter to match the gold in the cups or nonpareils to match the color of the patterned cups. Finish with a scattering of white chocolate curls (optional).

grate idea
Grate dark, milk, or white chocolate bars instead.

back to basics chocolate cupcakes p9... chocolate frosting p13...

rosebud romance

Always the choice for the timeless traditional wedding. What's more, these days, there is an astonishing array of beautiful handmade petal paste roses, now easily available from any cake-decorating or craft store.

for 24 cakes...

- ♡ 1 batch of Not So Little vanilla cupcakes in red foil cups
- ♡ 1 batch of vanilla buttercream frosting
- ♡ large size premade petal paste roses or rose buds
- ♡ star tipped pastry bag

1 Make up some vanilla frosting. For a wonderful added touch, add some rose extract to the frosting. Pipe a generous swirl on each cupcake.

2 Carefully embed one rose into the center of each cupcake.

3 Stand back and admire.

4 As an alternative, try lavender cups with a sprig of fresh lavender on top.

get real
Decorate the tables
with real rose petals
for a romantic effect.

back to basics vanilla cupcakes p8... buttercream frosting p12...

bridal tower

Cupcakes on a stacking tier with a small top bride and groom cutting cake to match are fast taking the place of traditional wedding cakes. It's easy to see why, when they look so stunning.

for the cutting cake and stacking cupcakes...

- ♡ 7½ in cake liners and 8 in cake pan for the cutting cake
- ♡ cupcake tier in rigid acrylic or plastic or glass
- ♡ buttercream frosting
- ♡ lilac food coloring
- ♡ petal paste
- ♡ silver edible glitter
- ♡ edible silver paint
- ♡ lilac sugar
- ♡ very large star and large star tips
- ♡ heart cutter
- ♡ pastry bag

The cutting cake

For the cutting cake: make a 6 oz, 3 egg cupcake batch. Mix and bake all the ingredients as a conventional cake, but in a liner so that, when cooked (40–45 minutes on 325°F), it will resemble a giant cupcake. Decorate the cutting cake and the cupcakes in exactly the same style, starting with a big lilac swirl of frosting. Make the hearts with cutters out of rolled-out petal paste, and allow to harden. Brush the hearts both sides with edible silver paint and drench with edible glitter. Position the hearts all over the cakes and sprinkle the frosting with lilac sugar.

The cupcakes

Make enough batches to allow one Not So Little or two Little cupcakes per guest. Following the photograph, decorate the cupcakes in exactly the same way but on a much smaller scale!

back to basics cupcakes p8... buttercream frosting p12...

more cupcakes for...

wedding favors

Wedding favors are a time-honored
tradition and, with these cute cupcakes,
they will be the talking point of the day.

white wedding

Match the color of the cake with your outfit
and accessories for a stylish coordinated look.
These traditional white cupcakes in classic ivory
boxes with complementary ribbon trimmings will
even match your dress!

pretty pastels

Add a touch of glamour to your wedding with a carefully chosen favor box to complement your cupcake embellishments. A stylish satin rose and sleek silver box enhances these delicate pink cakes and will really impress your guests. Alternatively, a pretty pastel favor box will simply add elegance to any color scheme.

first frost

Fans of "minimalist chic" will love these stylish white, blue, and silver cupcakes. Just make your cakes small and bite-sized to avoid unstylish crumbs!

for 48 cakes...

- ♡ 1 batch of Very Little vanilla cupcakes in plain cups
- ♡ 1 batch of white fondant icing
- ♡ blue icing
- ♡ rolled blue petal paste
- ♡ snowflake and reindeer cutters (or the shape of your choice)
- ♡ silver dragées

1 Carefully cover each cake with a cap of white fondant icing. For this look, take a little extra time to ensure a crisp, clean finish around the edge.

2 For the snowflakes and reindeer, press your shapes from rolled blue petal paste. Use a toothpick to help remove the shapes intact from their cutters.

3 Once dry, place them onto the cakes. If necessary, use a drop of watery confectioners' sugar to help them bond. Gently press a silver dragée into the center of the star.

cool tip
Try white frosting with blue sprinkles, as shown, for the same look—fast.

back to basics vanilla cupcakes p8... petal paste p16...

christmas morning

These stylish Christmas tree designs almost look like a bit of modern art—and you only need to learn how to pipe a squiggly line.

for 36 cakes...

- ♡ 1 batch of Little vanilla cupcakes in plain cups (or Christmas design cups)
- ♡ 1 batch of fondant icing
- ♡ royal icing
- ♡ green and red food coloring
- ♡ fine tipped pastry bag
- ♡ yellow star-shaped decorations

1 Spread a smooth, neat disk of white fondant icing to the edges of the cakes and allow to set.

2 Color your royal icing until you have the right "Christmas green" color and then pipe the tree in a continuous zigzag line, starting from the top.

3 Finish with a blob of red royal icing for the base and a yellow star sprinkle for the top.

festive bonus
Try piping a holly leaf, a bell, or a Christmas present.

back to basics vanilla cupcakes p8... royal icing p14... fondant icing p15...

tied up with ribbon

Bright and bold—these designs are striking and very versatile for many other gift occasions besides Christmas.

for 24 cakes...

- ♡ 1 batch of Not So Little vanilla cupcakes in red foil cups
- ♡ 1 batch of white fondant icing
- ♡ pink and red food coloring
- ♡ rolled fondant icing
- ♡ pink confetti decorations
- ♡ red nonpareils

1 Spread a smooth, neat disk of pale pink fondant icing to the edge of the cupcakes.

2 Roll out and cut strips of red fondant. Lay across cupcakes to make a loose unknotted bow. Cut the ends of each strip into a "V" for effect.

3 Finish with confetti sprinkles to enhance the decorative effect of the bow and then sprinkle with red nonpareils on to the pink icing to represent the design of the gift wrap.

christmas tip
Dust the board lightly with confectioners' sugar before rolling out your fondant.

back to basics vanilla cupcakes p8... fondant icing p15...

mistletoe kisses

These will be a lot of fun over the festive season. The idea is to lift up the little mistletoe plaque off the cupcake to get your Christmas kiss first. That's really having your cake and eating it!

for 24 cakes...

- ♡ 1 batch of Not So Little vanilla cupcakes in green foil cups
- ♡ 1 batch of buttercream frosting
- ♡ fine star tipped pastry bag
- ♡ petal paste
- ♡ mistletoe stencil
- ♡ small quantity of royal icing
- ♡ green coloring
- ♡ rolling pin
- ♡ metal spatula
- ♡ mother-of-pearl decoration balls

1 Roll out the petal paste and cut out small squares, or different shapes if you like, and allow to harden off.

2 Place mistletoe stencil on each petal paste plaque and apply a small quantity of stiff green royal icing across the stencil with a metal spatula to create the mistletoe picture.

3 Pipe a generous swirl of frosting on each cupcake. Place plaques on the cupcakes and complete with mother-of-pearl decoration balls for the mistletoe berries.

make a wish
If you don't have a stencil, pipe a twig of mistletoe with royal icing.

back to basics vanilla cupcakes p8... buttercream frosting p12... petal paste p16...

we three kings

These could well be the shining stars in your Christmas cupcake display—almost as precious as gold, frankincense, and myrrh themselves!

for 24 cakes...

- ♡ 1 batch of Not So Little vanilla cupcakes in gold foil cups
- ♡ 1 batch of royal icing with a variety of colors
- ♡ 1 batch of fondant icing
- ♡ small tipped pastry bag
- ♡ shiny edible decoration balls
- ♡ edible glitter

1 Prepare all the cupcakes with the three contrasting colors of icing, spreading a neat disk to the edge of each cupcake.

2 Choosing one color at a time, pipe the colored crowns on to each cupcake (try practicing on a plate first).

3 Finish with shiny balls and edible glitter.

star tip

Recreate the starry night with this colorful shooting star design.

back to basics vanilla cupcakes p8... royal icing p14...

perfect present

This is a nice idea for simple Christmas presents or token gifts, and you can make several at a time out of a batch of 48 cupcakes...

for 48 cakes...

- ♡ 1 batch of 48 Very Little vanilla cupcakes in a mixture of cups
- ♡ 1 batch of white fondant icing
- ♡ small quantity of petal paste
- ♡ several colorings
- ♡ shape cutters for bells, stars, baubles, and candles
- ♡ small cake boxes, about 4 in x 4 in x 2.5 in, preferably with a window lid
- ♡ white tissue and cellophane

1 First, spread a neat disk of white fondant icing to the edge of all your cupcakes and leave to harden off a little. Make the traditional Christmas decorative shapes—ideally pressed out of colored petal paste with cutters. If you don't have cutters, trace around suitable shapes with a sharp knife.

2 Place the shapes on the icing to suit the different-colored foil cups, and finish with a brushing of edible glue and glitter. Arrange an assortment of the different decorations into boxes of four, using the cellophane and tissue to present the cupcakes and cushion them in their box.

in the bag
Use clear or foil printed cellophane bags or boxes instead.

back to basics vanilla cupcakes p8... fondant icing p15...

more cupcakes for...

kids' christmas

These easily decorated cupcakes are ideal in the run-up to the festivities—no need for cutting out shapes from icing.

pick up a penguin
You should be able to find many inexpensive yuletide cake decoration motifs readily available in supermarkets in the run-up to Christmas.

polar bear
Transparent edible glitter gives a great polar-arctic feel to these comical cakes.

Using edible glitter is a
great way to add
a magical snowy
feel to cakes.

teddy bear

These could hardly be quicker to prepare—
just select some coordinating nonpareils or
edible glitter for a nice finishing touch.

mr frosty

White sanding sugar really enhances this
snowman scene, and the Christmas cupcake
cup designs are perfect.

christmas delights 119

acknowledgments

Our thanks in particular go to Ming Yee Shiu, our daughter Sophie, and our son Nigel, for their enthusiastic support and encouragement and practical help in setting up our website and kick-starting our cupcake business. Many thanks also to everyone at David & Charles—especially to Jenny Fox-Proverbs, for first suggesting to us that we should write this book.

suppliers

US

Candyland Retail Store
201 W. Main Street
Somerville
NJ 08876
Tel: 908 685 0410
www.candylandcrafts.com

New York Cake Supplies
56 West 22nd Street
New York
NY 10010
Tel: 800 942 2539
www.nycake.com

Wilton
Wilton Industries
2240 W. 75th Street
Woodridge
IL 60517
Tel: 630 963 1818
www.wilton.com

UK

Edsol Party Supplies
Edsol House
Buslingthorpe Green
Meanwood Road
Leeds L37 2HG
Tel: 01132 621122
www.edsol-party-supplies.com

Splat
P.O.Box 83
Princes Risborough
HP27 9WB
Tel: 0870 766 8290

Squires Group
Squires House
3 Waverley Lane
Farnham
Surrey GU9 8BB
Tel: 0845 225 5671
www.squires-group.co.uk

about the authors

Joan and Graham Belgrove left behind their careers in management and consultancy to launch The Little Cupcake Company Ltd in 2006 in response to the growing demand for unique celebration cupcakes. They now have an established internet business supplying cupcakes nationally to both private customers and major companies.

www.thelittlecupcakecompany.co.uk

index